The Night Before Christmas

Dorling Kindersley
LONDON, NEW YORK, SYDNEY, DELHI, PARIS,
MUNICH AND JOHANNESBURG

Produced by Leapfrog Press Ltd
Editors Naia Bray-Moffatt, Caryn Jenner
Managing Art Editor Miranda Kennedy
Art Editors Catherine Goldsmith,
Adrienne Hutchinson
Picture Research Liz Moore

For Dorling Kindersley
Senior Editor Alastair Dougall
Managing Art Editor Jacquie Gulliver
Senior Designer Lisa Lanzarini
Production Joanna Rooke, Linda Dare

First published in Great Britain in 2000 by
Dorling Kindersley Limited
9 Henrietta Street
Covent Garden, London WC2E 8PS

A CIP catalogue record for this book is available from the British Library.

ISBN 0-7513-2883-9

Colour reproduction by United Graphic Pte Limited, Singapore
Printed by L Rex in China

For our complete
catalogue visit
www.dk.com

The Night Before Christmas

Illustrated by
Anne Yvonne Gilbert

A Dorling Kindersley Book

Contents

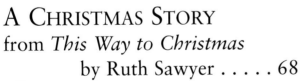

Introduction

♦

Celebrate "Christmas Dinner with the Cratchits" in an exerpt from
A Christmas Carol, *Charles Dickens' classic story, on pages 50-56.*

♦

Christmas means something special for everyone: the joy of holiday traditions; the excitement of Santa's visit; the pleasure of giving; hope for the future. This collection of stories and poems celebrates the Christmas spirit in all its forms. Included are a selection of Christmas favourites and other inspiring pieces that all brilliantly express the spirit of the festive holiday.

♦

Enjoy "A Visit from St Nicholas"
on pages 76-78.

♦

Each story is accompanied by a fascinating information page illustrated with colourful photographs from around the world. These information pages explore themes from the stories and give insights into different aspects of the Christmas holiday. Find out about Christmas celebrations in different places, and Christmases in past eras. Find out why we have Christmas trees, and who Santa Claus really was.

Find out about the Nativity on page 95.

◆

Christmas celebrates the birth of Jesus, who believed in love and goodwill. The stories and poems in *The Night Before Christmas* embrace the special love and goodwill of the season.

◆

The gifts for the "Twelve Days of Christmas" are on pages 58-60.

◆

We hope that you will celebrate the joy of Christmas with us in this collection, and we wish you a very happy Christmas!

◆

Read about Baboushka's special search on pages 80-94.

◆

The Cherry Tree Carol

JOSEPH WAS an old man,
and an old man was he,
When he wedded Mary,
in the land of Galilee.

Joseph and Mary walked
through an orchard good,
Where was cherries and berries,
so red as any blood.

Joseph and Mary walked
through an orchard green,
Where was berries and cherries,
As thick as might be seen.

O then bespoke Mary,
so meek and so mild:
"Pluck me one cherry, Joseph,
for I am with child."

O then bespoke Joseph,
with words most unkind:
"Let him pluck thee a cherry
that brought thee with child."

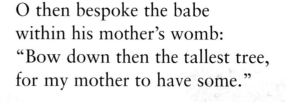

O then bespoke the babe
within his mother's womb:
"Bow down then the tallest tree,
for my mother to have some."

Then bowed down the highest tree
unto his mother's hand.
Then she cried, "See Joseph,
I have cherries at command."

O then bespoke Joseph:
"I have done Mary wrong.
But cheer up, my dearest,
and be not cast down."

Then Mary plucked a cherry,
as red as the blood,
Then Mary went home
With her heavy load.

Then Mary took her babe,
and sat him on her knee,
Saying "My dear son, tell me,
What this world will be."

"O I shall be dead, mother,
as the stones in the wall,
O the stones in the streets, mother,
shall mourn for me all.

"Upon Easter day, mother,
my uprising shall be;
O the sun and the moon, mother,
shall both rise with me."

The Little Fir Tree

HANS CHRISTIAN ANDERSEN

Retold by Alastair Dougall

FAR AWAY IN A FOREST a Little Fir Tree grew. The sun shone on him and gentle breezes played in his branches, but they gave him no pleasure. The birds sang and rosy clouds sailed overhead, but he thought nothing of them. Many other fir trees grew nearby, and children would sometimes come to the forest to play and look for wild strawberries. But though the Little Fir Tree was never lonely, he wasn't happy. If a child passing by said, "What a pretty little tree," the Little Fir Tree felt more miserable than ever.

All the Little Fir Tree ever thought about was growing up. "I wish I could be tall, like the other trees!" he used to sigh. "The birds would build their nests in my branches, and my top would look out over the whole wide world! And when the wind blew, I would bend my head and nod so grandly, like the tall trees do!"

In winter, when the ground glistened with snow, a hare would sometimes scamper along and jump right over the Little Fir Tree. This made him feel utterly miserable.

As time went by, the Little Fir Tree grew. When two winters had come and gone the hare could no longer jump over him, but had to walk around him instead. Still the Little Fir Tree wasn't satisfied. "If only I could grow tall and old," he thought. "That is the only thing worth living for!"

One autumn day, some woodcutters came to the forest and cut down some of the tallest fir trees. The Fir Tree, who was little no longer, shuddered as the tall trees tottered and crashed to the ground.

◆

*The hare could no longer jump over the Little Fir Tree,
but had to walk around him instead.*

◆

The woodcutters loaded the tall trees onto horse-drawn wagons, and took them far, far away from the forest.

The Fir Tree had no idea where the tall trees were going or what would happen to them. In spring, when the swallows and storks returned from faraway lands, he asked them if they knew.

The swallows knew nothing, but a stork said, "As I was flying over the sea from Egypt, I saw many ships. Some of them had fine new masts that smelt like fir. I'm sure that they were the trees that you speak of. They were stately, very stately, I assure you!"

The Fir Tree was impressed. "I wish I was tall enough to sail upon the sea!" he cried. "Tell me what the sea is like." But the stork said this would take far too long, and stalked off.

The woodcutters loaded the tall trees onto horse-drawn wagons, and took them far, far away from the forest.

"Enjoy being young while you can!" cried the sunbeams. And the wind gently ruffled the Fir Tree's branches and the dew wept gentle tears upon him. But the Fir Tree did not understand what they meant.

As Christmas drew near, the woodcutters came again to the forest. This time they cut down many trees, some of them not as tall as the Fir Tree. The woodcutters loaded the trees upon horse-drawn wagons and took them away.

"Those trees are no taller than I!" the Fir Tree cried. "Where are they going?"

"We know!" the sparrows twittered. "We looked through the windows in the town. We saw each tree planted in a warm room. Its branches were decorated with beautiful things: golden balls, sweets, toys, and candles!"

"What happened then?" asked the Fir Tree, trembling with excitement.

"Oh, we saw no more."

"What a wonderful fate – far, far, better than sailing over the sea," the Fir Tree exclaimed. "I wish that Christmas were here! I wish I could be one of those trees, standing proudly in a warm room, my branches decorated with beautiful things. And then – why something even grander must happen, or why would people take the trouble to decorate me? But what? I shall die of longing, I know I shall!"

♦

"We know!" the sparrows twittered. "We looked through the windows in the town.

♦

The air and the sunshine continued to care for him, whispering kindly, "Be happy, you are young, and free!" But the Fir Tree, desperate to become a Christmas Tree, took no notice of them.

The Fir Tree continued to grow – and by the next Christmas he was one of the handsomest trees in the forest, his branches clothed with dark green needles. He was one of the first trees chosen when the woodcutters arrived. As he was hauled off in the wagon, he suddenly felt sorry to be leaving his home in the forest.

The Fir Tree was taken, with many other trees, to a courtyard. He heard a man say, "This is a splendid one – just what we want!"

Two servants carried him into a spacious drawing-room, and set his trunk in a tub of sand. Then some young ladies, helped by their servants, decorated him with little nets cut from coloured paper, each net filled with sugar plums; with toffee apples and walnuts; with tiny dolls that seemed to dance among his branches. Here, there, and everywhere, they placed hundreds of candles, red, blue and white; and upon his very top they placed a star of gold tinsel.

"This evening," they cried,
"it will be lit up!" The Fir Tree
was so impatient for evening to
come that his bark ached!

Evening came at last and the
candles were lit, creating a blaze
of splendour. The drawing-room
doors were flung open, and in
rushed a troop of children,
followed by quieter, older
people. The children were
hushed by the Fir Tree's
glorious appearance, but only
for a moment. They were
soon dancing around the tree,
shouting with excitement.

"What will happen now?"
thought the Fir Tree anxiously.
As each bright candle
burned down, it was put out.
The children then flung
themselves upon the Fir Tree
and tore every present from
his branches, nearly knocking
him over. Only the gold tinsel
star remained; it was too
high up for anyone to reach.

◆

*The children were soon
dancing around the tree,
shouting with excitement.*

◆

When the children had found all the presents, a kindly-looking man told them a story about Humpty Dumpty, who, though he fell down, became king and married a princess. And so the evening ended peacefully.

In the morning the servants came in and the Fir Tree looked forward to being decorated again. But instead he was hauled out of the tub of sand, dragged up some stairs and dumped in a dark, cold attic.

Day after day the Fir Tree wondered why he had been put there; at last an answer came to him. "Of course," he thought. "It's winter and the ground is too hard to plant me. That's why I've been sheltered in here. People are so kind. A pity it's so dark, though. And so lonely."

Just then, some mice slipped in and out of his branches.

◆

The Fir Tree told the mice all about his life in the
forest, where the sun shines and the birds sing.

◆

"What are you doing here, old tree?" they squeaked.

"I am not old," the Fir Tree answered. "There are many trees older than I." And the Fir Tree told the mice all about his life in the forest, where the sun shines and the birds sing. The mice, who had seen nothing of the world, wanted to hear more about the forest, about the sun, the wind, and the gentle rain.

The Fir Tree found himself recalling every moment. "Those were happy times indeed," he thought sadly. "But they may come back, they may come back."

"What a life you have had, old tree!" exclaimed the mice.

"I am not old," the Fir Tree protested. "I only left the forest last winter!"

"Tell us a story," said the mice.

"I only know one, about someone called Humpty Dumpty. I heard it on the happiest evening of my life, though I did not know then how happy I was."

The Fir Tree told his one story, and told it well, for he could remember every word the kindly man had spoken on that golden Christmas Eve. The mice enjoyed it very much. However some rats, who had stopped to listen, sneered at the tale. "Don't you know a story about food?" they moaned.

"No," said the Tree. "That's the only one I know."

One morning some people came and cleared out the attic. The Fir Tree was dragged downstairs.

"Now my life begins again!" he thought, filled with hope as he was taken out into the fresh air and warm sunshine. He gazed at the beautiful flowers and the lime trees in blossom. Then he saw that his own branches were green no longer – they were dry, withered, yellow. Memories flooded his mind – of his happy forest life, of the merry Christmas Eve, and of the little mice who had listened so eagerly to the story of Humpty Dumpty.

"Past, all past!" the poor Tree sighed. "How I wish I had been happy, really happy when I had the chance."

He was thrown on a rubbish dump overgrown with weeds and nettles. The star of gold tinsel, which the Fir Tree had worn on the happiest night of his life was still stuck in his top. A group of children came by and the gold star caught the eye of the youngest, a boy who had danced around the Fir Tree on Christmas Eve. He took it and went to join his friends.

Later a servant put the Tree on a bonfire. And the Tree thought of summer days in the forest, of Christmas Eve, and of the tale of Humpty Dumpty, until it was nothing but ashes. Its story was over, just as all stories have to end. The children danced around the blaze. And on the chest of the youngest child sparkled the star of gold tinsel the Fir Tree had worn on the happiest night of his life.

On the chest of the youngest child sparkled the star of gold tinsel.

The Christmas Tree

Hans Christian
Andersen
(1805-75)

THE TRADITION OF DECORATING A FIR TREE put up in the home probably originated more than 400 years ago in Germany. The evergreen fir tree symbolized everlasting life, and the candles on it Jesus's love for the world.

The star on the top of the tree echoes the star that announced Jesus's birth.

Family fun
In Victorian times, Christmas trees became part of family celebrations all over the world. Prince Albert, the German husband of England's Queen Victoria, helped make them popular in Europe and America.

Presents galore
The Christmas tree is the bright centrepiece of many people's celebrations. Sometimes chocolates and sweets are hung on the tree, and presents put under it.

Bright lights
The Little Fir Tree by Hans Andersen tells of a tree who longs to become the glittering centre of attention at Christmastime.

Victorian market
At one time people used to go off to the forest for their trees, but as demand grew, trees were sold in markets. Buying one became a vital part of everyone's Christmas shopping!

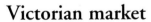

A Merry Christmas

LOUISA MAY ALCOTT

from *Little Women*

*Their father is away fighting in the American Civil War, money is scarce,
and the four March girls – Meg, Jo, Beth and Amy – have no presents to look
forward to at Christmastime. However, their mother has promised there will
be a little surprise waiting for them under their pillows when they awaken . . .*

JO WAS THE FIRST to wake in the grey dawn of Christmas morning.
No stockings hung in the fireplace, and for a moment she felt as
much disappointed as she did long ago, when her little sock fell down
because it was so crammed with goodies. Then she remembered her
mother's promise, and slipping her hand under her pillow, drew out
a little crimson-covered book. She knew it well, for it was *Pilgrim's
Progress*, that beautiful old story of the best life ever lived, and Jo felt
that it was a true guidebook for any pilgrim going the long journey.

She woke Meg with a "Merry Christmas", and bade her see what was under her pillow. A green-covered book appeared, with the same picture inside, and a few words written by their mother, which made their one present very precious in their eyes. Presently Beth and Amy woke, to rummage and find their little books also, one dove-coloured, the other blue; and all sat looking at and talking about them, while the East grew rosy with the coming day.

In spite of all her small vanities, Margaret had a sweet and pious nature, which unconsciously influenced her sisters, especially Jo, who loved her very tenderly, and obeyed her because her advice was so gently given.

"Girls," said Meg seriously, looking from the tumbled head beside her to the two little night-capped ones in the room beyond, "Mother wants us to read and love and mind these books, and we must begin at once."

◆

"Mother wants us to read and love and mind these books, and we must begin at once."

◆

"We used to be very faithful about it; but since Father went away, and all this war trouble unsettled us, we have neglected many things. You can do as you please; but I shall keep my book on the table here, and read a little every morning as soon as I wake, for I know it will do me good, and help me through the day."

Then Meg opened her new book and began to read. Jo put her arm around her and, leaning cheek to cheek, read also, with the quiet expression so seldom seen on her restless face.

"How good Meg is! Come, Amy, let's do as they do. I'll help you with the hard words, and they'll explain things if we don't understand," whispered Beth, very much impressed by the pretty books and her sisters' example.

"I'm glad mine is blue," said Amy; and then the rooms were very still while the pages were softly turned, and the winter sunshine crept in to touch the serious faces with a Christmas greeting.

"Where is Mother?" asked Meg, as she and Jo ran down to thank her for the gifts, half an hour later.

"Goodness only knows. Some poor creetur come a-beggin' and your ma went straight off to see what was needed. There never was such a woman for givin' away vittles, and drink, clothes and firin'," replied Hannah, who had lived with the family since Meg was born and was considered by them all more as a friend than a servant.

A bang of the door sent the girls to the table eager for breakfast.

"Merry Christmas, Marmee! Lots of them! Thank you for our books; we read some, and mean to every day," they cried, in chorus.

"Merry Christmas, little daughters! I'm glad you began at once, and hope you will keep on. But I want to say one word before we sit down. Not far away from here lies a poor woman with a little newborn baby. Six children are huddled into one bed to keep from freezing, for they have no fire. There is nothing to eat over there; and the oldest boy came to tell me they were suffering hunger and cold. My girls, will you give them your breakfast as a Christmas present?"

"My girls, will you give your breakfast as a Christmas present?"

They were all unusually hungry, having waited nearly an hour, and for a minute no one spoke; only a minute, for Jo exclaimed impetuously, – "I'm so glad you came before we began!"

"May I go and help carry the things to the poor little children?" asked Beth eagerly.

"I shall take the cream and the muffins," added Amy, heroically giving up the articles she most liked.

Meg was already covering the buckwheats[1], and piling the bread into one big plate.

"I thought you'd do it," said Mrs March, smiling as if satisfied. You shall all go and help me, and when we come back we will have bread and milk for breakfast, and make it up at dinner-time."

They were soon ready, and the procession set out. Fortunately it was early, and they went through back streets, so few people saw them, and no one laughed at the funny party.

◆

They went through back streets, so few people saw
them, and no one laughed at the funny party.

◆

[1] Buckwheats are a kind of pancake.

◆

*A group of hungry children cuddled under one old quilt,
trying to keep warm.*

◆

A poor, bare, miserable room it was, with broken windows,
no fire, ragged bed-clothes, a sick mother, wailing baby, and a group
of pale, hungry children cuddled under one old quilt, trying to keep
warm. How the big eyes stared, and the blue lips smiled, as the girls
went in!

"*Ach, mein Gott!* It is good angels come to us!" cried the poor
woman, crying for joy.

"We're funny angels in hoods and mittens," said Jo, and set
them laughing.

In a few minutes it really did seem as if kind spirits had been at
work there. Hannah had carried wood, made a fire, and stopped up
the broken panes with old hats, and her own shawl. Mrs March gave
the mother tea and gruel, and comforted her with promises of help.

Then she dressed the little baby as tenderly as if it had been her own. The girls, meantime, spread the table, set the children round the fire, and fed them like so many hungry birds; laughing, talking, and trying to understand the funny broken English.

"*Das ist gute! Der angel-kinder!*" cried the poor things, as they ate, and warmed their purple hands at the comfortable blaze. The girls had never been called angel children before, and thought it very agreeable. That was a very happy breakfast, though they didn't get any of it; and when they went away, leaving comfort behind, I think there were not in all the city four merrier people than the hungry little girls who gave away their breakfasts, and contented themselves with bread and milk on Christmas morning.

◆

There were not in all the city four merrier people than
the hungry little girls who gave away their breakfasts.

◆

Goodwill to All

People put donations in a wassail bowl. A 'wassail' is a toast or song.

CHRISTMAS IS A SPECIAL TIME to give thanks for our blessings, and to think of those who are less fortunate. You can show goodwill to all, through organized charities or small acts of kindness. As the March sisters learn, making others happy is the best way to share the Christmas spirit.

Christingle

Raise money for needy children at a Christingle service. The candle and the orange represent Christ's love for the world.

How you can help
Serve Christmas dinner at a homeless shelter; buy extra food for a needy family; donate toys to a children's home or hospital; or make an annual Christmas contribution to your favourite charity.

Victorian ladies made Christmas visits to the poor. In this picture, the footman brings in a hamper full of food.

Christmas carols

Singing Christmas carols is a fun and easy way to spread the joy of the holiday.Carollers bring Christmas cheer to hospitals and homes for the elderly. They can also sing carols in local neighbourhoods or shopping centres and collect charity donations.

Really, Truly, Reilly

ANNE MERRICK

O N THE NIGHT before Christmas the weather was cold and Samuel Shrubwort came home from work in a terrible temper.
When they heard him snarling through the hall, Oscar the cat, flimsy as a shadow, fled upstairs while Reilly, the small white dog with one black eye and one brown, slunk out of sight beneath the table.

"Scram!" bawled Samuel Shrubwort, giving the table a kick. "Get out, you HORRIBLE, SCRAWNY, USELESS dog!"

Useless? thought Reilly. Who's he calling useless? It's starving I am. Cold and uncared for as a long-buried bone. Really and truly, this is no life for a dog!

And seizing his chance while Samuel Shrubwort drank another tankard of beer, Reilly squeezed through Oscar's cat flap and escaped into the stone-cold winter street.

The weather was so cold that the stars shivered in the sky; so cold that all the trees turned white with frost and stood about the gardens like bony ghosts of themselves; so cold that in every house in Hometown, the fires burned with a blue flame.

"Heigh-ho," said Reilly. "On the night before Christmas, surely someone will give a home to a small white dog with one black eye and one brown."

And after a moment's thought he trotted up the hill to the Great Hall where the rich man lived.

On the night before Christmas, the rich man was counting his gold when he heard a sniffing and a scratching at his door.

◆

"Scram!" bawled Samuel Shrubwort, giving the table a kick.
"Get out, you HORRIBLE, SCRAWNY, USELESS dog!"

◆

"Help!" he cried.
"Thieves! Robbers!
Burglars! Bandits!"
"R-r-really!"
growled Reilly.
"I am not aBANDIT!
I'm just a small white
dog with one black eye
and one brown, and if
you give me a home I'll
guard your gold for you!"

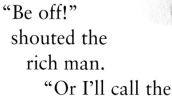

"Be off!"
shouted the
rich man.
"Or I'll call the
POLICE!"

Then he drew the bolt
across the door and the curtains across
the window, shutting off the warm and
friendly light.

Talk about giving a dog a bad name!
thought Reilly. Really and truly I wouldn't
want to live there anyway.

But he had a lonely kind of feeling
inside as he started back down the hill,
trying each house as he went.

To the man in the Church House he
protested, "I am NOT THE DEVIL
HIMSELF. I'm just a dog-in-need.
A lonely kind of dog. And if you give
me a home I'll do good works for you."

To the lady in the Pretty Pink Cottage, he pleaded, "But I am NOT A MANGY OLD FLEA-BAG! I'm just a lonely dog. A useful kind of dog. And I'll fetch your slippers for you if you'll only give me a home."

To the farmer in the Farmhouse, he barked, "What! WORRY YOUR SHEEP? Never! I'm just a dogged kind of a dog. A lonely, useful dog. And if you give me a home, I'll work my whiskers off for you!"

And to the innkeeper at the Welcome Inn, he howled, "Oh no I'm NOT A PESKY SCAVENGING STRAY. I'm just a dog-in-need. A dogged dog. A lonely, useful kind of a dog. Really and truly I'm used to drunks.

I'll chivvy them out and chase them home, if only you'll give me a bed and a bone!"

◆

*Only in the Small Shack
by the river a feeble candle
flame still flickered.*

◆

On the night before Christmas, by the time Reilly had gone
all the way down the hill, the curtains of every house in Hometown
were closed.

Only in the Small Shack by the river a feeble candle flame still
flickered. Reilly limped to the Shack and sat on the doorstep.
His paws were so caked with ice that he could not lift them to
scratch the door.

"Heigh-ho!" he sighed. "Here I am, a small white dog with one
black eye and one brown. A dog-in-need. A dogged dog. But there's
nobody in this world who will give me a home!"

And in spite of himself two tears rolled down his muzzle and froze
into pearls on his whiskers.

"Perhaps after all," he cried, "I'm a HORRIBLE... SCRAWNY...
USELESS... kind of a dog. A lonely, homeless dog."

Early on the morning of Christmas Day it snowed and soon all the
houses of Hometown lay snug under a dazzling white quilt.

Inside the Small Shack by the river Tim Merryweather stoked up the fire and he, his wife Lovejoy, and Jo-John their son, sat close around it. From a pot on the hob a warm smell of onion soup wafted up to the rafters. Tim Merryweather began to play the fiddle. He played the tunes of his favourite carols while Lovejoy sang the words. And on a patchwork blanket by the hearth, Jo-John stroked the head of a small white dog with one black eye and one brown.

"Tell me again," said Jo-John, "how he came to be my Christmas present – when I wasn't going to have any present…"

So Tim Merryweather rested his fiddle on his knee and told him how he'd just been saying his bedtime prayers when he'd heard a small sad cry outside.

◆

"Tell me again how he came to be my Christmas
present – when I wasn't going to have any present…"

◆

"And when I opened the door," he said, "I darn near fell over him. Frozen to the step he was! Dog-tired and nearly done for!"

Lovejoy stirred the pot of onion soup. "It seems to me," she laughed, "he must be a holy kind of a dog. Coming like that in answer to our prayers!"

Then Jo-John took from his pocket a morsel of the sausage he'd had for his breakfast and popped it into Reilly's grinning mouth.

"He's going to be my very best friend!" he said. "My one and only dog in the world!"

On the morning of Christmas Day, the small white dog with one black eye and one brown swallowed the sausage in one gulp.

"Really and truly," he said, "this is the life! And to think that only yesterday I was a horrible, useless, wholly lonely dog. And today I am the one-and-only-HOLY-kind-of-dog-in-the-world!"

And licking Jo-John's hand for the very last taste of the sausage, he winked his one black eye.

◆

"Really and truly," he said, "this is the life! And to think that
only yesterday I was a horrible, useless, wholly lonely dog."

◆

A Time for Giving

A Christmas pet like Reilly must be cared for all year round.

GIVING PRESENTS IS ONE OF THE joys of the holiday season. The first Christmas presents were actually presents given to Jesus when he was born. Now we celebrate the birth of Jesus by giving Christmas presents to loved ones.

In Britain, the postman received a gift on Boxing Day, the day after Christmas.

Christmas stockings

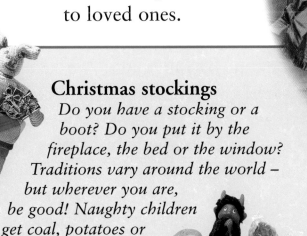

Do you have a stocking or a boot? Do you put it by the fireplace, the bed or the window? Traditions vary around the world – but wherever you are, be good! Naughty children get coal, potatoes or onions instead of a Christmas treat.

Americans often give homemade cookies.

The first Christmas presents

The Three Kings brought gifts for the baby Jesus. Melchior brought gold to honour Jesus as the King of Kings. Balthazar brought myrrh, an ointment used to embalm dead bodies. It was a sign that Jesus was going to die. Gaspar brought frankincense, an aromatic incense used in worship which showed the people that Jesus was God.

Gold　　Myrrh　　Frankincense

The Christmas Cherries

CHRÉTIEN DE TROYES

Translated by John Hampden

IN THE DAYS of King Uther Pendragon, who was King Arthur's father, there lived near Cardiff a noble knight named Sir Cleges. He was tall, good-looking and powerfully built, and he was wealthy too, for he owned many manors and farms. He spent all his money in helping others and there were many people who needed help, because the whole country was plagued by war. Many of the knights and barons fought among themselves, so that no one was safe and there was much suffering. Sir Cleges kept open house for anyone in distress, for he was the kindest, most hospitable of men, and every Christmas he gave a great feast.

❖

Sir Cleges spent all his money in helping others, and there were many people who needed help.

❖

He invited everyone, rich and poor, for miles around to his castle. You may be quite sure that after the feast Sir Cleges gave rich gifts, gold and silver, horses and clothing, to the minstrels who had entertained his guests by telling tales, such as this which I am telling you now.

For years the good knight lived happily in this way, with his gentle wife, Dame Clarice, and his two sons. But he grew steadily poorer. Yet he was too proud to change his way of life. He sold one manor after another to pay for all his hospitality, until he had only one manor left, and this was almost too small to keep him and his family. All their followers and servants deserted them one by one and they were left alone in miserable poverty.

When Christmas came round again Sir Cleges grew very sad, thinking of the feasts he had given, and his pride was humbled at last. He wept and wrung his hands and prayed aloud to God to have pity on him.

Dame Clarice heard that cry. She took him in her arms and said: "My lord, my dear love, it will not help us to mourn for the past. Let us thank God for all his gifts to us, for he has given us a great many. This is Christmas Eve, when everyone should rejoice. Come in to dinner, and let us do our best to be happy together."

What could Sir Cleges do but smile at her? They went in to their humble meal of bread and herbs, and made merry for their sons' sake all day.

He wept and wrung his hands and prayed aloud to God to have pity on him.

On Christmas morning they all went to church, and Sir Cleges felt much happier. Afterwards he went alone into his little garden, where he knelt on the grass under a cherry tree, thanking God with all his heart for God's gift of poverty. As he rose to his feet he put his hand on a low bough – and stood staring in amazement. The bough, the whole tree, which had been completely bare before, was now covered with green leaves and fine ripe cherries.

"Dear God," he cried, "what miracle is this?"

Plucking a large red cherry, he put it in his mouth. It was delicious. It was the best cherry he had ever tasted. He broke off a little bough laden with fruit and hurried into the house calling his wife: "My dear, my dear, look at this! Our cherry tree is covered with fruit. I am afraid it's a bad omen, it means more trouble coming to us."

His wife took the bough and marvelled at it, but her heart rose. "This is a good sign," she said. "This means better fortune for us.

◆

The whole tree was now covered with green leaves and fine ripe cherries.

◆

But whatever happens we will thank God for it." She thought for a moment. "Now let us fill a large basket with these wonderful cherries, so that tomorrow morning early you can set out for Cardiff with it, to give it to the king. He will be so astonished and pleased that he will give you a rich gift in return."

Sir Cleges kissed her and said: "I will do just as you wish."

At daybreak next morning he set out. He had not one horse left of the many which had once stood so proudly in his stables, so he had to use the "poor man's pony" – a strong staff – and his elder son went with him to carry the heavy basket of fruit.

When the two reached Cardiff Castle it was nearly dinnertime. Sir Cleges had been away from the court for so long that no one recognized him as he was now, old and worn, and wearing shabby clothes. When he and his son went in boldly at the main gate the porter stopped them at once.

"Churls," he said, "how dare you come in here! Get out!

◆

The porter stopped them. "How dare you come in here! Get out!"

◆

*The porter lifted the
lid of the basket.*

Otherwise, I'll break your heads
with my staff. Go and wait with the
beggars outside."

"Good sir," replied Sir Cleges
humbly, "I beg you to let me come in.
I have brought a wonderful present for
King Uther from the King of Heaven."

The porter lifted the lid of the basket,
and as soon as he saw the cherries he had
wit enough to realize that the king was
likely to give a rich reward to the bringer
of such a wonderful gift.

"By heaven," he said,
"you shall not come into the
castle unless you promise to
give me a third of anything
the king gives you, whether
it be gold or silver."

Sir Cleges could see
no hope of avoiding this,
so he said reluctantly,
"I promise," whereupon
the porter let him and
his son pass.

But they soon came
across the usher.

*But they soon came
across the usher.*

At the door of the great hall the usher stopped them, swinging his staff of office menacingly.

"You churls," he said, "what are you doing here? Be gone at once, or I will have you beaten from head to foot."

"Good sir," answered Sir Cleges meekly, "for the love of God do not be angry with me. I have brought the king a present from Him who created all things. See for yourself."

The boy brought the basket forward, and when the usher saw the cherries he could hardly believe his eyes.

"By St Mary," he said, "you shall not go into the hall unless you promise to give me on your way out a third of anything you may get."

Very sadly Sir Cleges gave his word, and he and his son made their way into the hall. It was full of lords and ladies, whose fine clothes made the poor knight look shabbier than ever. The king's steward came striding up angrily.

"How dare you enter the king's hall in those rags! Get out!"

But Sir Cleges stood his ground. "I have brought the king a wonderful present," he said, "from Him who died for our salvation." He lifted the lid of the basket and the steward stared and stared.

"By St Mary," he cried, "never in my life have I seen such a thing at Christmas."

◆

"How dare you enter the king's hall in those rags! Get out!"

◆

"This is a marvel indeed. I will not allow you to take it to the king unless you promise to give me a third of everything that the king gives you."

Sir Cleges was so cast down that he could not answer. He told himself sadly that all his trouble would go for nothing, for those three men would take everything.

"You rascal," growled the steward, "have you lost your tongue? Give me your promise at once or I'll have you beaten and flung out of the hall."

Sighing heavily, the poor knight replied, "You shall have a third of everything which the king may give me, I promise you."

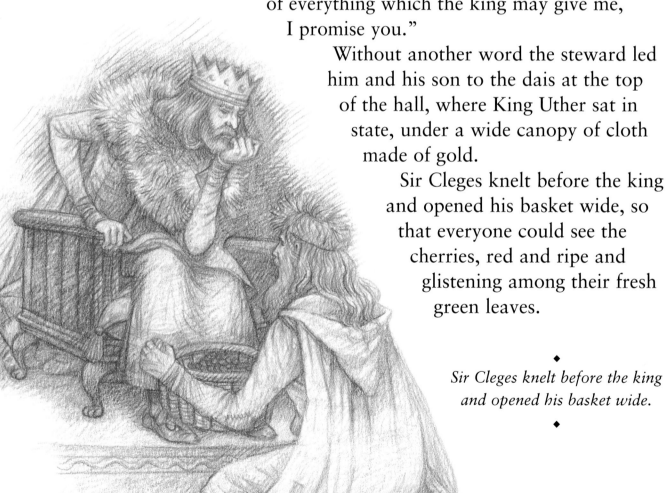

Without another word the steward led him and his son to the dais at the top of the hall, where King Uther sat in state, under a wide canopy of cloth made of gold.

Sir Cleges knelt before the king and opened his basket wide, so that everyone could see the cherries, red and ripe and glistening among their fresh green leaves.

◆

Sir Cleges knelt before the king and opened his basket wide.

◆

The trumpets sounded, and the feast began.

A silence fell. The fine lords and ladies looked at each other and looked again at the wonderful fruit. The king leaned forward to see the better.

"Sire," said Sir Cleges, "Our Saviour, Lord Jesus, has sent you these cherries by me."

"I give thanks to Him with all my heart," replied the king, "for this is a great marvel. Bring the basket here."

Sir Cleges put the basket in front of the king, who looked wonderingly at the cherries and ate two of them. "They are as delicious as they are marvellous," he said. "They shall be passed round so that everyone in this company can taste one of them, and you who brought them shall join our feast – and your son."

Sir Cleges and his son bowed low, and thanked the king, and then found humble places for themselves at one of the long trestle-tables which ran the whole length of that great hall. The king and the noblest of the court took their seats at the high table on the dais. The trumpets sounded, and the feast began.

There was rich food in plenty: all kinds of meat, fish and fowl, good wine and good ale, elaborate cakes and pastries, but for everyone present the crowning wonder was fresh, ripe, red fruit. For the rest of their lives they told the story of the Christmas cherries.

When the feast was over the king said to a squire: "Ask the poor man who brought the cherries to come to me."

Sir Cleges came at once and knelt on one knee before the king.

"You have done great honour to our feast and to me," the king said, "and I will reward you gladly. I will give you anything you ask, in gold or silver, goods or lands or anything else."

"Thank you, my liege," replied Sir Cleges, "but there is only one reward I wish: your gracious permission to give twelve blows with my staff to three men in this hall."

The king looked at him in astonishment. "You make me regret that I gave you that promise," he said. "Will you change your mind, and let me give you gold or perhaps precious stones from my treasury? Do you not need money?"

"Alas," said the knight sadly, "it would be of no use to me. All I ask is twelve blows."

"Then you must have my permission to give them, because I gave you my word."

Sir Cleges and his son bowed low once again. The king rose from the table, and as soon as he had left the hall the knight looked round for the steward.

There he was, at the far end of the hall, keeping watch at the great door. Grasping the heavy staff more tightly, Sir Cleges strode towards the door, and the steward turned to meet him.

"You are to give me one third of everything which the king gave you," he said harshly, "or I will have you whipped and take it all."

"The king gave me twelve blows," replied Sir Cleges, "and I will gladly give you your share." He swung his staff above his head. "One, two, three, four."

The steward howled in pain, and the bystanders laughed, for no one liked him, and Sir Cleges went on into the antechamber. The usher came scurrying after him at once, calling out: "Churl, churl, curses on you, give me my reward."

"Gladly," replied the knight. "Here you are. Five, six, seven, eight."

He went into the courtyard, towards the main gate, and at once the porter barred his way. "What did the king give you, churl?" asked the porter, glowering.

"Twelve strokes," the knight answered, "and you shall have your fair share. Nine, ten, eleven, twelve."

The last blow brought the porter to his knees.

◆

"The king gave me twelve blows," replied Sir Cleges, "and I will gladly give you your share."

◆

◆

Sir Cleges stopped at the door and listened in
amazement, for the minstrel was singing of him.

◆

Leaving him to the crowd, Sir Cleges went back to the great hall, with his son still close behind him.

The tables had all been cleared. A score of serving men were busy lifting them from their trestles, to be carried away, while others strewed fresh rushes on the floor.

The king was in his parlour, with a few of his lords and ladies, drinking spiced wine beside a blazing fire, while one of his court minstrels sang of knightly deeds.

Sir Cleges stopped at the door and listened in amazement, for the minstrel was singing of him.

When the song was finished the king gave a gold coin to the minstrel. "Sir Cleges was a brave and worthy knight," he said. "It is years since he came to court, and I miss him sadly. Where is he now?"

"I do not know," answered the minstrel. "He has gone away from this country."

Sir Cleges came forward, bowing to the king.

"Ah," said the king, "now tell me, why did you ask only for twelve strokes?"

The knight told him the whole story, and the king and all his courtiers laughed and laughed.

"This is a noble jest!" he said at last. "Bring the steward to me." And when the steward came, still rubbing his back, the king cried, "Well, Sir Steward, you got your desserts from this poor man. What have you to say for yourself?"

"May the devil fly away with him!" roared the steward. "I'll never speak to him again!"

The king laughed again, and said to the poor knight, "What is your name?"

"Sir Cleges, sire. As I hope for salvation, I am he."

"What!" cried the king. "Are you indeed that noble knight whom I have missed for so long?"

"Indeed, sire, I am. God has brought me low, as you see, but I am Sir Cleges."

"I see now that you are," said the king, "and I welcome you with all my heart. You shall not remain in poverty. I will make you governor of this castle of Cardiff and lord of all its lands. I will give you from my own treasury all the gold and silver that you may need, and you shall not leave me again."

"I thank you, sire," answered Sir Cleges, "and I thank God for the Christmas cherries."

"You shall not remain in poverty. I will make you governor of this castle of Cardiff and lord of all its lands."

Christmas Past

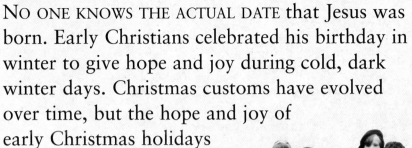

William Shakespeare included a Christmas elf in his play, As You Like It.

No one knows the actual date that Jesus was born. Early Christians celebrated his birthday in winter to give hope and joy during cold, dark winter days. Christmas customs have evolved over time, but the hope and joy of early Christmas holidays carries on.

Children bring home the Yule log in 1942.

Yule Log
For nearly a thousand years, people have continued the tradition of the Yule log by bringing home the biggest log possible. Burning the Yule log represents the sun and its warmth.

Christmas at the manor
Christmas was traditionally marked with a rowdy celebration. The entertainment featured court jesters, with much loud singing and marching round the banquet hall.

A soldier writes a Christmas letter home.

Christmas at sea
In the 19th Century, the main method of long-distance transport was by sea. Sailors often spent the holidays on board ship. This sailor is remembering Christmas 1879 by fixing a tree to the mast-head of the ship.

Christmas Dinner at the Cratchits

CHARLES DICKENS

from *A Christmas Carol*

The scene is Victorian London. Ebeneezer Scrooge loves only himself and values only money – until he is visited by the Ghosts of Christmases Past, Present and Future. Here, the Ghost of Christmas Present takes Scrooge to see his employee, Bob Cratchit and his family on Christmas Day. Scrooge's cold heart is warmed by the sight . . .

SCROOGE AND THE GHOST passed on, invisible, straight to Scrooge's clerk's; and on the threshold of the door the Spirit smiled, and stopped to bless Bob Cratchit's dwelling with the sprinkling of his torch.

Then up rose Mrs Cratchit, Cratchit's wife, dressed out but poorly in a twice-turned gown, but brave in ribbons, which are cheap and make a goodly show for sixpence; and she laid the cloth, assisted by Belinda Cratchit, second of her daughters, also brave in ribbons; while Master Peter Cratchit plunged a fork into the saucepan of potatoes. And now two smaller Cratchits, boy and girl, came tearing in, screaming that, outside the baker's, they had smelt the goose, and known it for their own; and basking in luxurious thoughts of sage and onion, these young Cratchits danced about the table.

"What has ever got your precious father then," said Mrs Cratchit. "And your brother, Tiny Tim; and Martha warn't as late last Christmas Day by half-an-hour!"

"Here's Martha, Mother!" said the girl, appearing as she spoke.

"Why, bless your heart alive, my dear, how late you are!" said Mrs Cratchit, kissing her a dozen times, and taking off her shawl and bonnet for her.

"We'd a deal of work to finish up last night," replied the girl, "and had to clear away this morning!"

"Well! Never mind so long as you are come," said Mrs Cratchit.

"There's father coming," cried the two young Cratchits, who were everywhere at once. "Hide Martha, hide!"

So Martha hid herself, and in came Bob, the father, with his threadbare clothes darned up and brushed, to look seasonable; and Tiny Tim upon his shoulder. Alas for Tiny Tim, he bore a little crutch, and had his limbs supported by an iron frame!

"Why, where's our Martha?" cried Bob Cratchit, looking round.

"Not coming," said Mrs Cratchit.

"Not coming!" said Bob. "Not coming upon Christmas Day!"

Martha didn't like to see him disappointed, even if it were only in joke; so she ran into his arms, while the two young Cratchits hustled Tiny Tim, and bore him off into the wash-house, that he might hear the pudding singing in the copper. His active little crutch was heard upon the floor, and back came Tiny Tim, escorted by his brother and sister to his stool beside the fire, while Bob compounded some hot mixture in a jug with gin and lemons.

*In came Bob, the father, with
Tiny Tim upon his shoulder.*

Master Peter and the two young Cratchits went to fetch the goose, with which they soon returned in high procession.

Mrs Cratchit made the gravy hissing hot; master Peter mashed the potatoes with incredible vigour; Miss Belinda sweetened up the apple-sauce; Martha dusted the hot plates; Bob took Tiny Tim beside him in a tiny corner at the table and the two young Cratchits set chairs for everybody.

At last the dishes were set on, and grace was said. It was succeeded by a breathless pause, as Mrs Cratchit prepared to plunge the carving-knife in the breast; but when she did, and when the long-expected gush of stuffing issued forth, one murmur of delight arose all around the board, and even Tiny Tim, excited by the two young Cratchits, beat on the table with the handle of his knife, and feebly cried "Hurrah!"

There never was such a goose. Its tenderness and flavour, size and cheapness, were the themes of universal admiration.

Eked out by the apple-sauce and mashed potatoes, it was a sufficient dinner for the whole family.

But now, Mrs Cratchit left the room to take the pudding up, and bring it in. A great deal of steam! The pudding was out of the copper. A smell like a washing day! That was the cloth. A smell like an eating-house, and a pastry-cook's next door to each other, with a laundress's next door to that! That was the pudding.

In half a minute Mrs Cratchit entered – flushed, but smiling proudly – with the pudding, like a speckled cannon-ball, so hard and firm, blazing in half-a-quartern[1] of ignited brandy, and bedight[2] with Christmas holly stuck into the top. Oh, a wonderful pudding! Bob Cratchit said that he regarded it as the greatest success achieved by Mrs Cratchit since their marriage. Everybody had something to say about it, but nobody said or thought it was at all a small pudding for a large family.

◆

Oh, what a wonderful pudding!

◆

[1] A quartern is a quarter of a pint.
[2] Bedight means adorned.

At last the dinner was all done, the cloth was cleared and the fire made up. Then all the Cratchit family drew round the hearth.

Bob proposed: "A Merry Christmas to us all, my dears. God bless us!"

Which all the family re-echoed.

"God bless us every one!" said Tiny Tim, the last of all.

He sat very close to his father's side, upon his little stool. Bob held his withered little hand in his, as if he loved the child, and wished to keep him by his side, and dreaded that he might be taken from him.

"Spirit," said Scrooge, "tell me if Tiny Tim will live."

"I see a vacant seat," replied the Ghost, "in the poor chimney corner, and a crutch without an owner. If these shadows remain unaltered by the Future, the child will die."

◆

"Spirit," said Scrooge,
"tell me if Tiny Tim will live."

◆

Scrooge cast his eyes upon the ground. But he raised them speedily, on hearing his own name.

"Mr Scrooge!" said Bob. "I'll give you Mr Scrooge, the Founder of the Feast!"

"The Founder of the Feast indeed!" cried Mrs Cratchit, reddening.

"It should be Christmas Day, I am sure, on which one drinks the health of such an odious, stringy, hard, unfeeling man as Mr Scrooge. I'll drink his health for your sake and the Day's, not for his!"

The mention of Scrooge's name cast a dark shadow on the party, which was not dispelled for full five minutes.

After it had passed away, Bob Cratchit told them how he had a situation in his eye for master Peter, which would bring in full five-and-sixpence weekly.

◆

"The Founder of the Feast indeed!" cried
Mrs Cratchit, reddening.

◆

Martha, who was a poor apprentice at a milliner's, then told them what kind of work she had to do, and how many hours she worked at a stretch.

All this time the chestnuts and the jug went round and round; and bye and bye they had a song from Tiny Tim.

There was nothing of high mark in this. They were not a handsome family; they were not well dressed; their shoes were far from being waterproof; their clothes were scanty; and Peter might have known, and very likely did, the inside of a pawnbroker's.

But they were happy, grateful, pleased with one another, and contented with the time; and when they faded, and looked happier yet in the bright sprinklings of the Spirit's torch at parting, Scrooge had his eye upon them, and especially on Tiny Tim, until the last.

When the Cratchits faded, Scrooge had his eye upon them, and especially on Tiny Tim, until the last.

Celebrations

In Brazil, the main Christmas dinner is traditionally eaten on Christmas Eve.

CHRISTMAS IS CELEBRATED by Christians around the world, although different countries follow their own customs. However, we are all celebrating the same special sense of hope and joy for the holiday season.

A candle ceremony, like this one in Portugal, is a magical experience.

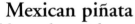

Mexican piñata
Children play with a papier mâché piñata. Each child is blindfolded before trying to open the piñata with a stick. When it finally breaks, sweets fly everywhere!

Treats from Britain
Christmas pudding and mince pies are made with fruits and spices. Mrs Cratchit's Christmas pudding is the highlight of dinner.

Girls in Scandinavia wear a crown of candles on St Lucia's Day.

Christmas parties
These children from Colombia make masks of Santa Claus. Other favourite party games include taking a "Lucky Dip" from Santa's sack of presents or giving "Secret Santa" gifts.

The Twelve Days of Christmas

THE FIRST DAY of Christmas,
My true love sent to me
A partridge in a pear tree.

The second day of Christmas,
My true love sent to me
Two turtle doves and
A partridge in a pear tree.

The third day of Christmas,
My true love sent to me
Three French hens,
Two turtle doves and
A partridge in a pear tree.

The fourth day of Christmas,
my true love sent to me
Four Colly birds,
Three French hens,
Two turtle doves and
A partridge in a pear tree.

The fifth day of Christmas,
my true love sent to me
Five gold rings, Four Colly birds,
Three French hens,
Two turtle doves and
A partridge in a pear tree.

The sixth day of Christmas,
my true love sent to me
Six geese a-laying,
Five gold rings,
Four Colly birds,
Three French hens,
Two turtle doves and
A partridge in a pear tree.

The seventh day of Christmas, my true love sent to me
Seven swans a-swimming, Six geese a-laying,
Five gold rings, Four Colly birds,
Three French hens,
Two turtle doves
And a partridge in a pear tree.

The eighth day of Christmas, my true love sent to me
Eight maids a-milking, Seven swans a-swimming,
Six geese a-laying, Five gold rings,
Four Colly birds, Three French hens, Two turtle doves
And a partridge in a pear tree.

The ninth day of Christmas, my true love sent to me
Nine drummers drumming, Eight maids a-milking,
Seven swans a-swimming, Six geese a-laying,
Five gold rings, Four Colly birds,
Three French hens, Two turtle doves,
And a partridge in a pear tree.

The tenth day of Christmas,
my true love sent to me
Ten pipers piping,
Nine drummers drumming,
Eight maids a-milking,
Seven swans a-swimming,
Six geese a-laying, Five gold rings,
Four Colly birds,
Three French hens, Two turtle doves
And a partridge in a pear tree.

The eleventh day of Christmas,
    my true love sent to me
    Eleven ladies dancing, Ten pipers piping,
      Nine drummers drumming,
      Eight maids a-milking,
        Seven swans a-swimming, Six geese a-laying,
        Five gold rings, Four Colly birds,
          Three French hens, Two turtle doves and
          A partridge in a pear tree.

The twelfth day of Christmas, my true love sent to me
Twelve lords a-leaping, Eleven ladies dancing,
Ten pipers piping, Nine drummers drumming,
Eight maids a-milking,
Seven swans a-swimming,
Six geese a-laying,
Five gold rings,
Four Colly birds,
Three French hens,
Two turtle doves and
A partridge in a pear tree.

The Christmas Season

CHRISTMAS IS MORE THAN JUST one day of the year. People begin preparing and celebrating well before Christmas Day. In fact, Christmas Day is only the first day of the holiday. As "The Twelve Days of Christmas" shows, Christmas actually lasts for 12 days, finishing on January 6.

Advent calendars mark the days from December 1 until Christmas Eve.

Twelfth Night
Traditionally, Twelfth Night was celebrated with boisterous masquerade parties. Guests performed comic sketches and wassailed the trees, toasting them with songs.

Holiday greetings
The first mass-produced Christmas card was sold in England in 1843.

Christmas at the theatre
The holiday season means special excitement at the theatre. *The Nutcracker*, shown here, is a famous ballet about a girl's toys coming to life at Christmastime. Pantomimes are traditional Christmas entertainment in Great Britain. Audience participation at 'pantos' is definitely encouraged!

Christmas lights
Christmas lights remind people of the bright star that was seen on the night Jesus was born.

The Cat on the Dovrefell

PETER CHRISTEN ASBJØRNSEN AND JORGEN I. MØE

Retold by Neil Philip

ONCE ON A TIME there was a man up in Finnmark who had caught a great white bear, which he was going to take to the King of Denmark. Now, it so fell out that he came to the Dovrefell just about Christmas Eve, and there he turned into a cottage where a man lived, whose name was Halvor, and asked the man if he could get house-room there, for his bear and himself.

"Heaven never help me, if what I say isn't true!" said the man, "but we can't give anyone house-room just now, for every Christmas Eve such a pack of Trolls come down upon us that we are forced to flit, and haven't so much as a house over our own heads to say nothing of lending one to anyone else."

"Oh?" said the man, "if that's all, you can very well lend me your house; my bear can lie under the stove yonder, and I can sleep in the side-room."

Well, he begged so hard that at last he got leave to stay there; so the people of the house flitted out and before they went, everything was got ready for the Trolls; the tables were laid and there was rice porridge and fish boiled in lye[1] and sausages and all else that was good just as for any other grand feast.

[1]Lye is a white alkaline solution.

So, when everything was ready, down came the Trolls. Some were great and some were small; some had long tails; and some had no tails at all; some too, had long, long noses; and they ate and drank, and tasted everything. Just then, one of the little Trolls caught sight of the white bear, who lay under the stove. So he took a piece of sausage and stuck it on a fork and went and poked it up against the bear's nose, screaming out: "Pussy, will you have some sausage?" Then the white bear rose up and growled and hunted the whole pack of them out of doors, both great and small.

Then the white bear rose up and growled.

Next year Halvor was out in the wood on the afternoon of Christmas Eve cutting wood before the holidays, for he thought the Trolls would come again; and just as he was hard at work, he heard a voice in the wood calling out:

"Halvor! Halvor!"

"Well," said Halvor, "here I am."

"Have you got your big cat with you still?"

"Yes, that I have," said Halvor. "She's lying at home under the stove, and what's more, she has now several kittens, far bigger and fiercer than she is herself."

"Oh, then, we'll never come to see you again," bawled the Troll away in the wood, and he kept his word; for since that time the Trolls have never eaten their Christmas brose[1] with Halvor on the Dovrefell.

✦

*"Then we'll never come to see you again,"
bawled the Troll.*

✦

[1]Brose is a kind of porridge.

Tales and Traditions

MANY CHRISTMAS TALES AND TRADITIONS have been inspired by the nativity story. But others stem from ancient celebrations of the winter solstice, which, in the northern hemisphere, marks the end of winter and the coming of spring.

In the Italian legend, La Befana is a witch who rides her broomstick in search of the baby Jesus. At Christmas, she brings gifts for the "holy children" in every home.

Evergreen plants such as holly represent the beauty of nature all year round.

Mummers
Mummers can still be seen in parts of England on Christmas Eve and Twelfth Night. They perform funny adaptations of famous legends, such as Saint George fighting the dragon.

Fancy dress
"The Cat on the Dovrefell" takes place in Scandinavia. Children in the Scandinavian countryside visit neighbouring farms for cakes and sweets. They wear fancy dress to scare away winter spirits and welcome back the sun.

The Holly and the Ivy

THE HOLLY and the ivy,
When they are both full grown,
Of all the trees that are in the wood,
The holly wears the crown.

The rising of the sun
And the running of the deer,
The playing of the merry organ,
Sweet singing in the choir.

The holly bears a blossom,
As white as any flower,
And Mary bore sweet Jesus Christ,
To be our sweet Saviour.

The holly bears a berry,
As red as any blood,
And Mary bore sweet Jesus Christ,
To do poor sinners good.

The holly bears a prickle,
As sharp as any thorn,
And Mary bore sweet Jesus Christ
On Christmas day in the morn.

The holly bears the bark,
As bitter as any gall,
And Mary bore sweet Jesus Christ
For to redeem us all.

The holly and the ivy,
When they are both full grown,
Of all the trees that are in the wood,
The holly bears the crown.

There's Snow on the Fields

THERE'S SNOW on the fields,
And cold in the cottage,
While I sit in the chimney nook
Supping hot pottage.

My clothes are soft and warm,
Fold upon fold,
But I'm sorry for the poor
Out in the cold.

A Christmas Story

RUTH SAWYER

From This Way to Christmas

THIS IS THE STORY the gypsy mothers tell their children on the night of Christmas, as they sit round the fire that is always burning in the heart of a Romany camp.

It was winter – and twelve months since the gypsies had driven their flocks of mountain-sheep over the dark, gloomy Balkans[1], and had settled in the southlands near the Aegean. It was twelve months since they had seen a wonderful star appear in the sky and heard the singing of angelic voices afar off.

They had marvelled much concerning the star until a runner had passed them from the South bringing them news that the star had marked the birth of a Child whom the wise men had hailed as "King of Israel" and "Prince of Peace".

This had made Herod of Judea afraid and angry and he had sent soldiers secretly to kill the Child; but in the night they had miraculously disappeared – the Child with Mary and Joseph – and no one knew whither they had gone.

Therefore Herod had sent runners all over the lands around the Mediterranean with a message forbidding everyone to give food or shelter or warmth to the Child, under penalty of death. For Herod's anger was far-reaching and where his anger fell, his sword fell also.

[1] The Balkans is an area of southeastern Europe. It is bordered by the Aegean Sea.

Having given his warning, the runner passed on, leaving the gypsies to marvel over the tale they had heard and the meaning of the star.

Now on that day that marked the end of the twelve months since the star had shone, the gypsies said amongst themselves: "Dost thou think that the star will shine again tonight?"

It was true, what the runner said, that when it shone twelve months ago it marked the place where the Child lay. It might even mark his hiding place this night. Then Herod would know where to find Him, and send his soldiers again to slay Him. That would be a cruel thing to happen!

The air was chill with the winter frost, even there in the southland, close to the Aegean; and the gypsies built high their fire and hung their kettle full of millet, fish and bitter herbs for their supper.

The gypsies built high their fire and hung the kettle for their supper.

The king lay on his couch of tiger-skins and on his arms were amulets of heavy gold, while rings of gold were on his fingers and in his ears. His tunic was of heavy silk covered with a leopard cloak, and on his feet were shoes of goat-skin trimmed with fur.

Now, as they feasted around the fire a voice came to them through the darkness, calling. It was a man's voice, climbing the mountains from the south.

"Ohe! Ohe!" he shouted. And then nearer, "O-he!"

The gypsies were still disputing among themselves whence the voice came when there walked into the circle about the fire a tall, shaggy man, grizzled with age, and a sweet-faced young mother carrying a child.

"We are outcasts," said the man hoarsely. "Ye must know that whosoever succours us will bring Herod's vengeance like a sword about his head. For a year we have wandered homeless and cursed over the world. Only the wild creatures have not feared to share their food and give us shelter in their lairs. But tonight we can go no farther; and we beg the warmth of your fire and food enough to stay us until the morrow."

◆

"We beg the warmth of your fire and food enough to stay with us until the morrow."

◆

The king looked at them long before he made reply. He saw the weariness in their eyes and the famine in their cheeks.

He saw, as well, the holy light that hung above the child, and he said at last to his men: "It is the Child of Bethlehem, the one they call the 'Prince of Peace'. As yon man says, who shelters them shelters the wrath of Herod as well. Shall we let them tarry?"

One of their number sprang to his feet, crying: "It is a sin to turn strangers from the fire, a greater sin if they be poor and friendless. And what is a king's wrath to us? I say bid them welcome. What say the rest?"

They gathered round the child to touch his small hands and feel his hair.

And with one accord the gypsies shouted, "Yea, let them tarry!"

They brought fresh skins and threw them down beside the fire for the man and woman to rest on. They brought them food and wine, and goat's milk for the child; and when they had seen that all was made comfortable for them they gathered round the child to touch his small hands and feel his hair. They brought him a chain of gold to play with and others for his neck and tiny arms.

"See, these shall be thy gifts, little one," said they, "the gifts for thy first birthday."

And long after all had fallen asleep the child lay on his bed of skins beside the blazing fire and watched the light dance on the beads of gold.

He laughed and clapped his hands together to see the pretty sight they made; and then a bird called out of the thicket close by.

"Little Child of Bethlehem," the bird called, "I too, have a birth gift for thee. I will sing thy cradle song this night." And softly, like the tinkling of a silver bell and like clear water running over mossy places, the nightingale sang and sang, filling the air with melodies.

The nightingale sang and sang, filling the air with melodies.

And then another voice called to him. "Little Child of Bethlehem, I am only a tree with boughs all bare, for the winter has stolen my green cloak, but I also can give thee a birth gift. I can give thee shelter from the biting north wind that blows." And the tree bent low its branches and twined a roof-tree and a wall about the child.

Soon the Child was fast asleep, and while He slept a small brown bird hopped out of the thicket. Cocking his little head, he said: "What can I be giving the Child of Bethlehem?"

"I can give thee shelter from the biting north wind that blows."

*The small brown bird spread his wings and
caught the sparks on his own brown breast.*

"I could fetch Him a fine fat worm to eat or catch Him the beetle
that crawls on yonder bush, but He would not like that! And I could
tell Him a story of the lands of the north, but He is asleep and would
not hear." And the brown bird shook its head quite sorrowfully.

Then it saw that the wind was bringing the sparks from the fire
nearer and nearer to the sleeping Child.

"I know what I can do," said the bird joyously. "I can catch the
hot sparks on my breast, for if one should fall upon the child, it would
burn Him grievously." So the small brown bird spread wide his wings
and caught the sparks on his own brown breast.

So many fell that the feathers were burned; and burned was the flesh beneath until the breast was no longer brown, but red.

Next morning, when the gypsies awoke, they found Mary and Joseph and Child gone. For Herod had died, and an angel had come in the night and carried them back to the land of Judea. But the good God blessed those who had cared that night for the Child.

To the nightingale He said: "Your song shall be the sweetest in all the world, for ever and ever; and only you shall sing the long night through."

To the tree He said: "Little fir tree, never more shall your branches be bare. Winter and summer you and your seedlings shall stay green, ever green."

Last of all He blessed the brown bird: "Faithful little watcher, from this night forth you and your children shall have red breasts, that the world may never forget your gift to the Child of Bethlehem."

◆

*"From this night forth you and your
children shall have red breasts."*

◆

Animals at Christmas

ANIMALS ARE AN IMPORTANT part of Christmas. Sheep, cows and oxen were all present in the manger in Bethlehem when Jesus was born. "A Christmas Story" shows that the goodness of Jesus touched all living things. And indeed, the robin, with his bright red breast, has become a well-known sign of Christmas cheer.

The robin is a symbol of Christmas.

The dove represents the spirit of peace.

The helpful donkey

A donkey carried Mary to Bethlehem, where she gave birth to Jesus. In those times, donkeys were a common form of transport for poor folk.

Saint Francis of Assissi

Saint Francis is the patron saint of animals. In this picture, he preaches to the birds. Like Jesus, he believed in the goodness of all creatures.

Santa's reindeer

In many countries, Santa's sleigh is traditionally pulled by reindeer. The reindeer in this picture are tended by a shepherd in Siberia, in northern Russia.

A Visit from Saint Nicholas

CLEMENT C. MOORE

"TWAS THE NIGHT before Christmas, when all through the house
Not a creature was stirring, not even a mouse.
The moon, on the breast of the new-fallen snow,
Gave a lustre of midday to objects below;
When what to my wondering eyes should appear,
But a miniature sleigh and eight tiny reindeer,
With a little old driver, so lively and quick
I knew in a moment it must be St Nick.
More rapid than eagles his coursers they came,
And he whistled and shouted and called them by name:
"Now, Dasher! Now, Dancer! Now, Prancer and Vixen!
On, Comet! On Cupid! On, Donner and Blitzen!
To the top of the porch, to the top of the wall!

Now, dash away, dash away, dash away all!"
As dry leaves that before the wild hurricane fly,
When they meet with an obstacle, mount to the sky,
So up to the house-top the coursers they flew,
With a sleigh full of toys – and St Nicholas, too.
And then in a twinkling I heard on the roof
The prancing and pawing of each little hoof,
As I drew in my head and was turning around,
Down the chimney St Nicholas came with a bound.
He was dressed all in fur from his head to his foot,
And his clothes were all tarnished with ashes and soot.
A bundle of toys he had flung on his back,
And he looked like a pedlar just opening his pack,
His eyes how they twinkled! His dimples how merry!
His cheeks were like roses, his nose like a cherry;
His droll little mouth was drawn up like a bow,
And the beard on his chin was as white as the snow.

The stump of a pipe he held tight in his teeth,
And the smoke it encircled his head like a wreath.
He had a broad face, and a little round belly
That shook, when he laughed, like a bowl full of jelly.
He was chubby and plump – a right jolly old elf –
And I laughed when I saw him, in spite of myself.
A wink of his eye and a twist of his head
Soon gave me to know I had nothing to dread.
He spoke not a word, but went straight to his work,
And filled all the stockings; then turned with a jerk,
And laying his finger aside of his nose,
And giving a nod, up the chimney he rose.
He sprang to his sleigh, to his team gave a whistle,
And away they all flew like the down of a thistle;

Santa Claus

Saint Nicholas is the patron saint of children.

THE POPULAR IMAGE of Santa as jolly and plump with twinkling eyes and a snow-white beard comes from the poem "A Visit from Saint Nicholas", published in 1822. The author, Clement Clark Moore, wrote the poem to entertain his children on Christmas Eve.

Jultomten is the Swedish Santa Claus.

A modern Santa roller skates in Florida.

The original Saint Nicholas
Nicholas was a bishop in Turkey. He saved three poor sisters from slavery when he secretly threw three bags of gold down the chimney into their house.

Santa Claus, Sinter Klaas

Santa has many names. In fact, Santa Claus is derived from the Dutch *Sinter Klaas*. In France, he is called *Père Nöel*; in Japan, *Santa Kurohsu*. In Germany, he is *Christkindl* (Christ child).

Santa joins a river parade.

Baboushka

ARTHUR SCHOLEY

"WHAT DID I tell you? It's twice as big as last night!"
"But what does that mean, old man?"
What else can it mean? It's coming this way, of course.
The star is coming this way!"
The excitement sped through the village like a wind.
All came out of the houses to gaze upwards.
All came out – except Baboushka. She banged about,
and swept her house, polishing, scouring, and shining.
"Hey – Baboushka!"
"What's that?" – clattering, pulling up carpets.
"Come out here. Look at this!"

"What on earth is it?" –
pushing chairs about.

"Nothing on earth, Baboushka!
Up in the sky!"

"I'll look through my window.
Whereabouts?"

"Towards the mountain, towards
the East."

They waited, marvelling.

"Can you see it?"

"Oh! What a dirty window. And I washed
it this morning."

"Look though the window, Baboushka!" they laughed.

"Oh, yes," she said. "Very nice. Well, I must get on."

No wonder her house was the best kept, the best polished,
washed, and painted. Her garden was beautiful, her cooking superb.
You had to wear your best clothes, polish the soles of your shoes if
she invited you in for a meal.

"It's just a star!" she muttered. "They'll let the slightest thing put
them off." She paused, just for a second, remembering the stars
reflected, dancing once, in the eyes of a baby. "No use dreaming
about that," she bustled. "Work to do."

Far into the night she worked, to make up for the wasted time.

But the next day, the village still twittered and speculated. The
star could not be seen in the sunlight but all agreed that it was still
there. The night would show it, and so it did. The star loomed
towards them, brighter than the moon.

"Definitely, it's moving."

"It's blue!" "No, it's red!" "Green and purple!"

"Looks orange to me, definitely orange."

"I'm frightened!" "Don't be silly, Narinka."

Clatter went a window. Out came a mop, vigorously shaking. Down showered dust and bits.

"Oh! Baboushka!"

"What, who's that?"

"My hair's filthy with dust!"

"What are you doing under my window at this time of night?" Out came her head. "Is it a holiday?" she asked.

"It's the star!"

"What, again? If any of you have time to spare, come and beat my carpets for me. I've all my cooking to do tomorrow and I want to make an early start." Crash, down came the window again.

Baboushka baked and cooked, spread, chopped, and sprinkled. The loaves were crisp, the cakes miraculous, the meat pies and pasties, buns and scones sang as they came out of the oven.

No one else worked that day. A message had come. Who had received it? No one knew. What was the message? An army was on the way. No, not an army – a procession of all the rulers of the world.

Twilight had hardly begun before gasps were heard.

The star was overhead, sparkling with all colours, mysterious, awe-inspiring.

A silence fell on all. They gazed and gazed; old men got cricks in their necks; children lay on their backs and got dizzy. Only in the small hours did the street finally empty. Then, hardly had they got to sleep, when a cry came with the dawn:

"They're coming!" "Wake up!" "Come and see!"

Out came all the villagers again and stumbled towards the mountain road. A twinkling string of lights could plainly be seen coming down the pass. In the far distance could be heard the sound of pipes, the tinkling of bells…

In two hours, and full morning light, the procession entered the village.

The procession entered the village.

The villagers lined the street, open-mouthed at what they saw.

First came the piper on a pony. Horses followed bearing heavily hooded men, each carrying brass-bound caskets. Dogs ran in and out; several men were walking, trudging wearily, ignoring the crowds.

"Who are they? What do they want?" The questions died as they saw the magnificence of the three proud horse-riders, for these, surely, were – "Kings, kings!" whispered the villagers.

And they certainly looked like kings even though they were cloaked against the dawn mist.

The first was in a red cloak and a hat, all trimmed with fur. He had a long white beard and rode a brown horse. The second wore a blue velvet cloak and a rose-coloured turban. He had a dark beard and rode a silver horse. The third, on a prancing black horse, was dressed in grey and gold and silver. His eyes twinkled as he looked at the villagers.

◆

"Kings, kings!"
whispered the villagers.

◆

They stopped. One of the heavily hooded men dismounted and approached the villagers. They shrank back.

He laughed. "Do not be afraid. My masters" – he indicated the three proud riders – "seek a place to rest until evening. Where is the hostel, or is there an inn?"

They eagerly told him the bad news. There was no hostel. There was a tavern where they drank at nights, but this, alas, was closed.

Where, then, was the next village? Down the path, they told him, about twenty miles. Weariness overcame the servant's smile. He went back, bowed, and exchanged a few words with the three riders.

He came back to the group of waiting villagers. "My masters say: Is there not anywhere they can stay here? Will anyone offer hospitality? Just shelter, warmth?"

He smiled at the villagers in turn. The idea astonished, then appalled them. Into whose home could these magnificent people go? Where was there any place fit to receive them?

Then, in a second, of course they knew – Baboushka!

They led the way to her house.

"What is it now?" she demanded, throwing open the door and gaping in wonderment at the faces, and especially at the three royal personages who dismounted and waited.

"Lady," said the servant, "we seek your kindness, your hospitality. We have travelled all night, and must go on this evening. Would you offer my masters here shelter and warmth, just for the daylight hours?

Baboushka gulped, nodded, and threw open the door wide.

◆

"Will anyone offer hospitality?"

◆

The three rich riders bowed to her and passed into the bright, clean-as-a-new-pin home. They sat in her polished chairs, threw off their cloaks in the warmth of her glowing fireside. In came servants.

Outside, the villagers now offered their homes to the rest of the travellers. They took and groomed the horses, boiled water, prepared meals, heard things to make their eyes grow big, and their ears flap, and their tongues wag for years to come.

Baboushka seemed possessed by a demon. She whipped out the cloths, the dishes that were never used (but she knew they were clean) and laid before them all she had prepared the day before.

Their eyes sparkled at home-made bread, meat pies, cakes, jam, pickles, food fit for a king but never offered to them in their rich palaces. They ate heartily and, in between her dashing here and there, up and down, in and out, she found out, through the day, who they were and why they were making their journey.

They were kings, she learned, and they were following that Star. But where to? And why? They didn't know where, they told her. All they could do was follow it through the night. They believed that the Star would lead them to a new king, they said, a king such as the world had never seen before.

"Why seek a new king?" Baboushka asked. "You are kings yourselves, are you not?"

"We are kings," said the first king, who was called Melchior, "but our kingdoms are small. The king we seek, is, we think, to be king of Earth and Heaven. This we infer from the glory of his Star."

"The Star was foretold," said Gaspar, the second king. "We have it in our records and they agree. So we joined up to follow it."

"What is the King's name?" she asked.

"Even this we do not know," answered Gaspar. "Perhaps he does not yet have a name. After all he will be but a few days old."

"Then he's a baby!" cried Baboushka.

◆

*Their eyes sparkled at home-made bread, meat pies,
cakes, jam, pickles, food fit for a king.*

◆

"Why yes," they smiled.

"A baby? And yet king of Earth and Heaven?" she said.

Melchior smiled, raised his hands, shrugged his shoulders.
"All we have to go on is the Star. And that, I am sure you will
agree is magnificent."

"So why," said Balthasar, the third king, suddenly, "why don't
you come with us, and see this king for yourself, eh?"

"I?" said Baboushka, astonished.

"Why not?" urged Gaspar. "Bring him a gift, as we do. I bring
gold, my colleagues spices, precious ointments."

Baboushka laughed. "It would be better to give a baby toys."

Melchior sighed. "There, you see?" He turned to his companions. "Toys! We never thought of it. It needs a woman to think of such things. Toys! Of course. But we set out so hurriedly," he added. "As soon as the Star appeared."

"But you have toys?" Gaspar asked in surprise. "Have you, perhaps, children?"

Baboushka looked away. "I had a baby," she said. "He was the king of my life, but he died. This is why, perhaps, I feel a desire to see your king."

"Our king? Everyone's king. Yours, too," said Melchior.

"So you are coming with us this evening?" asked Balthasar.

"Oh!" said Baboushka. "I don't think I'll be ready tonight. There's so much to do. I'm not prepared for travelling. And I'll need to prepare gifts."

Melchior smiled. "The day is before you," he said. "If you'll excuse us now, we ought to try to sleep while we have the chance."

All day Baboushka laboured. There was all the washing and putting away of dishes for a start; then all the cooking had to be done again, for most of the week's supply had gone. She had hardly time to think about a journey, but, at odd moments, she daydreamed about the new king, about the baby who had just been born.

During the afternoon, she had a couple of minutes between the baking and cooking. She went to a cupboard in a small room at the back of the house, and peered inside. There, under films of dust, were toys of all kinds – some of them new, the rest barely used. Tears came into her eyes.

Then she thought of the new baby king. He shall have the lot, she decided. She couldn't take the toys like this, of course. They would all need to be cleaned, polished.

Suddenly she shut the door. She smelt the cooking. She rushed into the kitchen, opened the oven. Ah, just in time!

Throughout the afternoon she considered going with the kings on their journey, but it seemed more and more difficult to her. What would she wear? It would depend on how long the journey would be, and no one seemed to know that.

Also, she would need to spend some time cleaning the house when her visitors had finished their sleep. She couldn't just leave it like that and go off. What would it be like to return to a dirty house – after how long?

The light faded into dusk. The red piper could be heard as he slowly walked the length of the street. Out of the houses came the servants. The horses were brought and the sound of restless hooves echoed on the stones.

The piper came to the end of his tune. "The Star! The Star is there, lords," he called, "and it is moving on."

Baboushka entered the room and curtseyed. "You will eat before you go?"

"Thank you, lady, no," said Gaspar. "We must be on our way."

"The Star is moving on," said Melchior. "We must follow it."

"Are you ready?" asked Balthasar, and all the three kings waited, looking at Baboushka.

Baboushka sighed. "I will follow on later," she said. "I'm not ready. There is so much to do. Later, tonight, when I have done all I have to do, I will catch you up. There will still be the Star."

"Yes," said Balthasar, "but it does move quickly. And suppose you don't catch us up?"

"The people on the way will tell me which way you have gone," Baboushka pointed out.

"All is ready, masters."

The three kings bowed to Baboushka. The servant handed her a bag of money. Quickly the kings mounted their horses. The piper began his melody and the procession moved on.

The villagers waved and cheered as the procession wended its way down the valley. The Star shone ahead of them.

How Baboushka worked! What a mess there seemed to be. She bustled in and out, sweeping, dusting, beating cushions and carpets. Next came the clearing up in the kitchen after her day of cooking.

Eventually she opened the special cupboard and took out the toys. Some would need scrubbing; others required careful dusting; some ivory animals would need washing gently; a gold and silver trumpet would have to be polished. There was more work here than even she had realized.

She started at once. One by one the toys shone good as new, bringing with them memories of the child for whom they had been prepared. On she worked until they were all fit to give to a Royal Baby.

Now, how was she to carry them? She packed the toys in her biggest basket. She looked through the window, surprised to see that it was getting light. It couldn't be dawn, could it? But it was.

Clear on the air came the sound of the farm cockerel.

She dashed out into the street and looked up. The Star had gone! But of course, it couldn't be seen in daytime, and that was why the kings rested then. There was ample time to catch up.

She rushed back into the room. Goodness, she had had no rest for a day and night, and there was the prospect of a day's journey before her. She was exhausted. Perhaps if she rested, just for an hour?

She sank onto the bed, and slept.

She woke suddenly. She had only been asleep a few moments, she thought. Then she saw that it was dark. It couldn't be that she had slept all day. But that is what she had done.

She ran into the street. She was horrified. She couldn't see the Star anywhere in the sky. She ran back into the house, pulled on her cloak, picked up the toys and stuffed a few clothes into a bag.

Out into the street she came, locking the door behind her. She hurried down the path, in the direction the kings had gone. As she went she knew in herself a great desire to see the baby king. Now it seemed to be the most important thing in the world.

In the next village she enquired about the kings. Yes, the kings had passed this way. On she went, hurrying, urgently. She passed through village after village. The days passed and she lost count of them. The villages grew bigger and became towns; still it was easy to get news about the kings. So she went, never stopping, through night and day until she came to the city.

This is where the baby king would be, for here there was talk of a palace.

But when she enquired, the guard was irritated at her question. "First those foolish kings, and now you," he snapped. "They've gone."

"But where? Where?" she begged.

"Well, now, I did hear … no, the name is on the tip of my tongue … isn't it funny how you can forget?" Baboushka realized what the man was after. She delved into the kings' bag, took out a coin, handed it over. "Ah, yes, now I remember," he said. "Bethlehem! That was the place." He looked at the bag. She gave him another coin. "And you'll find it in that direction. It's quite a way," he added. Baboushka set off at once. "It's only a village!" the guard called after her. "You won't find a king there."

She knew she dare not stop, except to ask directions. Soon she had left the city and begun to climb up a steep, winding path.

She came into Bethlehem towards evening. How could there be a royal baby here, she thought. It was a ramshackle place, quiet, only a few houses, rather like her own village, except that this one did have an inn. The kings would have stayed there, she supposed.

"Yes," the landlord told her, "the kings came two days ago, but they didn't stay and this was as well, since the place was packed because of the census. They had money and I was quite prepared to throw one or two people out. But they had taken it into their heads to go off suddenly, and so –"

"But what happened to the baby?" Baboushka cried.

"Ah, yes," said the landlord. "The kings wanted to see the baby. Can't think why." He stopped, seeing Baboushka's face. "If you like," he said quickly, "I'll show you where the baby was. Come on."

He took down a lantern and she followed him across the yard to the stable. "There!" he said. "I couldn't offer anything better. I told you the place was packed full." The animals stared at them. "They put the child in the manger," the innkeeper laughed, as he left.

Baboushka knelt down at the manger. Here was where the baby had lain. The place was cold, dark, and the animals were restless. What could she do now, but go back? There was nothing left for her.

"Baboushka?"

She jumped up, startled. Someone stood there in the half light of the doorway. He looked kindly at her.

"Do you know anything of the baby that was here?" she asked.

"I do. I have just seen the Holy Family off on their journey to Egypt and safety," he said.

"And the kings?" asked Baboushka.

◆

Someone stood there in the half light of the doorway.

◆

"They returned to their kingdoms by another road to avoid the king of the city. But they told me of you. I am sorry that you are too late. The shepherds who were here earlier, they came as soon as they received the message. The kings came as soon as they saw the Star. It was the Christ Child they found, the world's Saviour."

Baboushka wept, clutching her basket of toys in the cold stable.

"Baboushka?" The figure came nearer. "I am to tell you that you will find the child, if you go on searching. But do you want to?"

"Oh yes, yes!" said Baboushka. "There is nothing for me now but to find the Christ Child if I can."

"You have chosen, then. God will go with you. Go in peace."

The angel smiled and stood aside, pointing through the open door. And Baboushka began her search, and entered into the legend.

It is said that she is looking still, for time means nothing in the search for things that are real. Some say that it is only when the world ends and time comes round again that Baboushka will find the Christ Child and be the first to kneel.

In the meantime, year after year, she goes from house to house, calling: "Is he here? Is the Christ Child here?"

Particularly at Christmas, when she sees a sleeping child and hears of good deeds, she will lift a toy from her basket and leave it there, just in case.

Then on she goes, still seeking, still crying: "Is he here? Is the Christ Child here?"

The Nativity

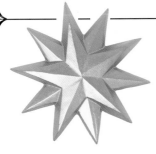

A bright star shone in the sky to announce the birth of Jesus to the world.

THE NATIVITY IS THE STORY OF the birth of Jesus. When Mary and Joseph arrived in Bethlehem, the town was crowded and there was nowhere to stay. Mary knew that the baby was going to come soon. At last, an innkeeper offered his stable. It was in the stable that Jesus was born.

Mary rested, while Joseph watched over the baby Jesus.

Shepherds saw the star. Then an angel told them that the Saviour had been born.

Nativity crib

Saint Francis of Assissi (p75) recreated the birth of Jesus in the 13th Century using real people and animals. Many people now make models of the Nativity.

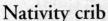

The three kings

The three kings in the story of Baboushka travelled to Bethlehem to give their gifts to the baby Jesus. They arrived on the 12th day of Christmas, which is called Epiphany. The three kings are also known as the three wise men or *magi*.

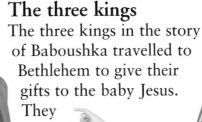

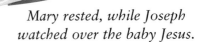

Acknowledgements

The publishers would like to thank the copyright holders for their kind permission to reproduce the following copyright material:

"Really, Truly, Reilly", copyright © 1990 by Anne Merrick. Reproduced by permission of Oxford University Press. "The Christmas Cherries", by Chrétien de Troyes. Translated by John Hampden. Reproduced by permission of J M Dent & Sons. "The Cat on the Dovrefell" by Peter Christen Asbjørnsen and Jorgen I. Møe. Retold by Neil Philip. "A Christmas Story", copyright © 1944 by Ruth Sawyer from *This Way to Christmas*. Reproduced by permission of Harper & Row. "Baboushka", copyright © 1979 by Arthur Scholey. First published by Rex Collings.

Every effort has been made to obtain permission to reproduce copyright material, but there may be cases where we have been unable to trace a copyright holder. Dorling Kindersley will be happy to correct any omissions in further printings.

The publishers would also like to thank the following for their kind permission to reproduce photographs.

t = top; b = bottom; l = left; r = right; a = above; c = centre

AKG London: 19bl, 79cr; Bridgeman Art Library: 19tl, tr, 49bl, 65tl, 75cr, 79tr / Gavin Graham Gallery: 19br / Stapleton Collection: 57cl, 61tr; Bruce Coleman Collection: 65c, 75c, cl; Collections: 27cl, 57cr, 65cr; Sue Cunningham: 57tl; Catherine Ashmore/Dominic Photography: 61b; Mary Evans Picture Library: 27tl, bl, 35tr, 49tl, c, br, 65b, 79tl / Children's Society: 49tr; Robert Harding Picture Library: 79cl; Hutchinson Library: 79br; Press Association: 27cr; South American Pictures: 57c, br; Tony Stone Images: 57tr, 61cl, 75tl, b.

Additional photography by Andy Crawford, Barnabas Kindersley, Dave King, Diana Miller.